MW00414723

How to Start an
Etsy Online Business

The Handmade Creative Entrepreneur's Guide

Jill b.

Table of Contents

Introduction

I'll admit that I'm not particularly artistic but I've been crafty for as long as I can remember. I used to make intricate cross-stitch and crochet pieces with no possibility of selling or making money on my crafts (I was a child of the '80s). These days however, we have so many opportunities to make our wares available to a worldwide audience. How amazing is that?

I am an entrepreneur. I have been selling on eBay and the now defunct Yahoo Auctions since 1998. I later branched out to selling on Amazon as well. Even though I discovered Etsy in 2006, I didn't start selling on the platform until 2012 when I started selling our reinvented chicken saddle (refer to the author bio at the end of the book if you're interested in learning more). I am a creative entrepreneur.

Unfortunately, many creatives don't like to think of business and money and might even feel like they're "selling out". If you're reading this book, I'm going to assume that you are a creative entrepreneur as well. Otherwise, you need to work on shifting your mindset. You can be both an artist or creative as well as a business person. Think of your sales as, "Wow, someone loved my work enough to buy it from me!" How cool is that?

Setting Business Goals

Today, instead of having the only option of opening a storefront or in-person venue to sell your creations, you can set up your digital storefront with relative ease and low start-up costs. That is a wonderful advantage when you're starting out. Although there are new selling platforms like Handmade by Amazon coming up, at the time of writing, Etsy is still by far the best and largest platform for crafters and artists to sell their wares online.

Before you get too excited however, remember that this also means that the entry point is low for everyone else as well. Yes, some stores Etsy shops can make tens of thousands of dollars a month on Etsy but these are established businesses who got in at an earlier stage. As more and more people flood into the market and with new Etsy rules allowing wholesaling and pre-manufactured items, it has become harder to gain a foothold.

Don't despair. That doesn't mean that you can't still start a business. You just need to be realistic about business volume and sales, especially when you're new. More importantly, you need to figure out *what* you want from your business.

Do you just want to just sell some of the items you've made or are planning to make?
Do you just want to make a little extra pocket money?

Do you want to generate a side income to help pay the bills? Or, do you want something more, like having a business that will replace a job? Where do you see your business and brand a year from now? What about 5 years from now?

There are no right or wrong answers and your aspirations can change over time as you and your situation change. However, having goals in your mind will help you to formulate the steps you need to take in order to achieve those goals.

Brand YOU

In this noisy market, I believe one of the best ways to stand out from the crowd is to distinguish your brand or your business from others. Whether you're making the items or selling vintage items or craft supplies, what make you, *you*? Remember that people shop on Etsy because they generally want to find something different. Otherwise, they would have shopped at Amazon, eBay or your local big box store.

What makes your brand stand out? Do they promote something? Is it how you see the world? Are your works a reflection of your childhood or your experiences or just the things you like? Whether it's bringing ethnic native craft supplies from around the world or 1950s kitsch to your customer or whether it's the nature that inspires your artwork, selling something that is meaningful to you will help to give your business a sense of purpose while helping it stand out from the crowd.

Note though, that this book assumes that you're selling quality items with good workmanship. negative review can have longstanding effects on your brand and business so make sure that you test your products in real-world situations. If you make crocheted scarves, wear one to make sure it will withstand the rigors of weather and wear. Make kids' toys? Have some relevantly-aged kids test them out for you in actual play situations. We tested our product on our chickens for about a year before as launched it to market.

Your Product Line

Once you've narrowed down your niche, figure out your target audience. Who is going to buy your products? Are they generally young, single women? Moms-on-the-go? Business women? Most of Etsy's audience are women but that doesn't mean you can't sell masculine products. It just means that you probably want to target your products to a female audience. Think gifts wives, mothers or girlfriends may buy for the men in their lives instead of targeting men themselves.

You can then plan to offer product lines that either have a common look or feel, or form recognizable or complementary sets. For example, you may choose to just focus on selling a knitted hats. You may later wish to branch out and offer matching scarves and gloves.

Avoid selling a jumble of items like vintage toy cars and jewelry for example. I'll be honest and admit that I made this mistake when I started selling on Etsy. Because my background was selling on eBay, I was used to just throwing up whatever items I'd found to flip for a profit. With a reputation of being an online flea market of sorts, selling in this way on eBay worked fine for me. However, this doesn't translate to an Etsy audience. It wasn't until much later when I started learning about branding, that this is a big mistake. An odd selection of items will confuse your customer and mess your branding up.

If you have unrelated products that you really want to offer for sale, it will be a good idea to have separate shops for them. You can always invite customers to visit your other shop. For example, if you sell knitted clothing, you may also want to point customers to your jewelry store.

In addition to offering complementary products, in time, you may also want to try to hit different markets at different price points. For example, you may be selling original art pieces for hundreds or thousands of dollars. You can stretch the product line by offering art prints and postcards. You may also want to offer digital downloads, which allows buyers on a budget to print your work themselves. Digital downloads are on the lower-end of the price scale but a business like this can be scaled up almost definitely since you don't have to invest additional time or effort to fulfil orders once the system is set up.

On the flipside, you may want to scale up product lines. For example, if you sell essential oils, you can add other products like handmade soaps, candles and lotions using your essential oils. The possibilities are endless if you plan appropriately.

Comparing Your Product(s) to Others on the Market

Once you have an idea of the products that you want to sell, do some research. Look on Etsy, Pinterest and even Instagram to see what similar products others are selling. I can almost guarantee you that there is already some kind of iteration of the product or products that you are planning to sell. Some products may be lesser to yours while others may be better.

Doing your product research will give you a better idea of what works and what doesn't. Do some color combinations work better than others? Are there certain shapes or sizes that seem to sell more? Make note of all these characteristics. You can even make your own secret Pinterest (http://pinterest.com) board or save your notes on websites like Evernote (http://evernote.com) to help you keep things organized.

Then, pick out successful shops and compare your products against theirs with an impartial eye. How can you make yours stand out better such that it'll spur customers to buy? I'm not telling you to copy anything but rather, learn from what you see. Then, come up with your own unique spin on things.

Getting Organized

When it comes to a very hands-on business like selling on Etsy, streamlining your production and business process is extremely important. Once you've figured out your business goals and your expected product line, you'll need to figure out how to best work it into your schedule.

Streamlining will not only help you save time but money, especially when it comes to ordering supplies and raw material. Generally, if you place one big order from a distributer, you'll not only save on shipping cost but may also have more bargaining power. Never assume that posted prices are fixed. Ask if you can get any discounts or price breaks.

Of course, you need to balance between streamlining but not overstocking inventory, which also costs money. Unfortunately, I don't have any fixed answer as to how much to stock. It will really depend on demand as well as your storage space constraints. My best advice would be to not stock too much at first, then slowly scale up as you see sales increase.

Collecting all your items together before you start selling on Etsy also means that you can make a production line out of the selling process. This includes taking photos and writing descriptions. The more related items you have for sale, the more likely the chance of someone buying one or more of your items. I recommend aiming to have at least 20 different items for sale at any one time.

I'll admit however, that I don't follow this practice on my Etsy storefront. I only have a few item options for sale there, mostly because the goal of my Etsy storefront is just to try to capture some of Etsy's customer base. Otherwise, I always drive sales to my own storefront. I'll go into more details as to why in a later chapter.

Things You Will Need to Get Started

Besides the tools and materials needed to make your products and access to Etsy, these are some of things you'll need to get your Etsy business started:

Time. In addition to the time you'll need to make your products, you'll also need to factor in time you'll need to set up and take product photos, listing items, interacting with customers, packing and shipping. It'll help if you allocate certain times to do certain things like taking product photos on a Saturday morning (when there's good natural light), and preparing shipments (which needs relatively less mental energy) in the evenings.

Regardless, all these facets of running an Etsy business can take up a lot of time so if you have a full-time job, be prepared to set aside weekends and nights to making this business happen, especially if you want to make a full-time living.

A Paypal and bank account. A Paypal is helpful to have but is not essential because Etsy also offers a "Direct Checkout" option where it processes payments for you, even if you don't have a Paypal account. If you have a Paypal account, you can also opt for streamlining the checkout process. That means that even if a buyer uses Paypal to pay, the funds will be swept into your Etsy account. It will then be deposited into your registered bank account at scheduled intervals.

The plus side to this is that you don't have to keep logging into Paypal to mess around with payments. However, you also cannot immediately sweep Paypal payments into your bank account if you use the streamlined process. Funds are deposited every Monday unless you use the *Schedule* option.

A good camera and photography stage with appropriate, preferably natural lighting. Your photo stage should be simple and match the theme of your products. For example, if you sell jewelry inspired by the sea, picturing your product against a backdrop of sand would match the theme without distracting from the products themselves. Try to minimize shadows as much as possible. If all else fails, consider using a lightbox which you can either buy or make yourself.

A photo editor is recommended. Adobe Photoshop and Lightbox will by far give you the most functions, options and filters. However, for quick touchups, you can also use free online photo editors like http://pixlr.com. Gimp (http://gimp.org) is another photo editing software that is free to download and use.

A dedicated work area. Depending on what you're making, this area can range from a small table to entire rooms. If you have the space, it would also be a good idea to have an area dedicated to processing your shipping. This is where you'll store all your shipping supplies like packing tape, supplies, a printer for shipping labels (optional but recommended) etc.

Packing supplies -- like packaging material, packing tape, paper for printing etc. It is also good to have a printer for printing shipping labels etc.

Shipping scale (digital is recommended). For small items, you can use a digital kitchen scale in a pinch.

Access to a shipper (USPS/UPS/Fedex).

Setting Up Your Business Entity

The following suggestions are for informational purposes only. These are the steps that I have taken with my business. I am not a lawyer, financial or tax professional. You should consult your local legal and tax professional if you need specific advice about setting up your business.

If you're planning on selling on Etsy or any other venue seriously, you might want to consider setting up a separate company entity. You can register your corporate entity status through your Secretary of State's website.

Once you have a business established through your state, you can apply for an Employer Identification Number (EIN) though the IRS (http://1.usa.gov/1hBUiLt). An EIN is a tax identification number which is separate from your personal social security number. The process is quick and easy and can be done for free online. The IRS will issue you an EIN almost immediately. You can use your EIN for all your business transactions including your paypal and business bank account information. You will also need to use your EIN when you file tax returns for the business.

Etsy Names

Etsy allows you to have three types of names to represent yourself on the platform: username, real name and shop name.

The username is the name you use to register your Etsy account with and cannot be changed. It, or your email, is also what you use to log into your account with. The username is made public unless you add your full name, in which case the full name replaces the username in almost all places on Etsy.

While revealing your name is optional, it'll help show your customers that there's an actual person behind the shop. I just use the initial of my last name to retain a little bit of privacy. However, if you use your full name, it'll be easier for people who already know you to find you. While the full name cannot be a business name, in addition to initials, you can also use a nickname. If you have a team running your shop, you can use multiple names as well.

Finally, there's the shop name, which is the name that represents your Etsy business. It is also the name that is used in the URL: http://www.etsy.com/shop/*shopname*. When choosing a shop name, again, try to choose a name that represents your products or brand that is narrow enough to give buyers an idea of what you sell, but not so focused that you confine yourself.

For example, shop names like "womanshopsworld" (selling beads and craft supplies from all over the world), "LinkedByAThread" (selling embroidered goods), and "sewmuchfrippery" (selling vintage sewing patterns) all at minimum, hint at what the shop sells. Their names also allow for a focused range of goods.

Ideally, you also want to add a keyword search term into your name as well like "sew", "crochet", "woodwork" or "lotions" etc. That way, when someone types in that search term, your shop name will pop up as well. Remember that your shop name is not set in stone and you can tweak it. However, it's best to come up with a final name as quickly as possible.

Before settling on a name, make sure that it is available on other platforms and social media as well. You want to keep your brand name consistent across the board. Knowem.com (http://knowem.com) is a good site which will check for name availablity on a wide range of websites, including the most popular social media sites. It also searches for trademarks but I would also check the US Patent & Trademark Office (http://hyperurl.co/uspto) to see if that name has already been trademarked or not.

Opening Your Shop

The setup process is pretty easy. Over time, Etsy's interface may change and evolve but the idea remains the same. At the top right of the site, click on "Sell on Etsy" (https://www.etsy.com/sell) or "Open a shop" on the bottom left.

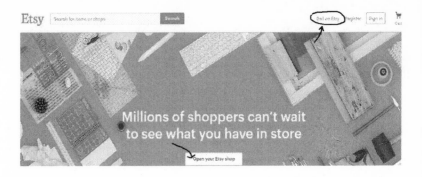

You can register manually or use your Facebook or Google+ login information. Next, select your shop language, country, and currency. The shop language is different from your preferred language. That is, you may prefer to view Etsy in one language but your shop language is the language that your customers will see. Then add your shop name.

Listing Your Item

Photos

Don't be fooled by Etsy's handmade-homemade vibe. Gone are the days where a crappy photo is good enough. In this fast-paced environment, your item only has a few seconds to make an impression. Otherwise, people move on to the next item. Nice images are your chance to make that first good impression. It shows potential customers that you are a professional and take your products seriously.

Fortunately, with today's technology, you don't need expensive equipment or have a professional photographer to get beautiful, perhaps even stunning images. You don't need the most expensive camera in the world to take nice photos but having a decent one would be a good start. Generally, a DSLR (digital single-lens reflex) camera with a larger sensor offers you more control and will capture better light than a smartphone or point-and-shoot camera.

If you're selling tiny items, dainty jewelry or need to take a lot of closeups to show detail, you might need to use a camera with a specialized macro lens. Otherwise, having a camera that has a built-in image stabilizer or using a tripod will also help to keep the image steady. If you want to produce an image when it's in focus but the background is blurred, use a wider aperture setting (f/1.8 or f/2.8).

If you're using a light box, set it up in a section of your work-area that has good light and a clean background. You can purchase a light box of make your own. Youtube has some videos on how to make one cheaply.

Photography is its own skillset. Using full auto settings doesn't always do the final shoot the most justice. Experiment with different manual camera settings (aperture, shutter speed and white settings) to help you to figure out what works best in your lighting. Generally though, it's best to let your camera autofocus. Unless you're very good a focus, the camera will do a better job at it.

Next, experiment with props, models and composition. Some items, like hats, scarves and socks look better on a model than on their own. If you're selling a painting, photograph is hanging on a wall so that customers can visualize how it will look against home decor. Try to keep your branding consistent in all the product line photos. For example, you may want to use the same model, or have some sort of color of background element or motif that ties everything to your brand. This will help to give a cohesive feel to your shop.

A good way to get a feel of your photos is to check the shots on your photo editor before moving on. That way, you can see on your screen what worked and what didn't then, adjust lighting or re-compose your image and reshoot as needed. It is a lot easier to correct the set up a physical shoot as it happens than to try to make serious edits in your photo editor.

In terms of photo-editing functions, Photoshop with Lightroom is by far the most versatile. However, its subscription pricing model can become pricey in the long run. Other photo editing options include Pixlr (http://pixlr.com), Gimp (http://gimp.com) and PicMonkey (http://picmonkey.com).

Photoshoots are a time-consuming process so taking photos of as many items as possible in that session will help to save a lot of time and streamline the selling process. Don't be too hard on yourself in the beginning. It takes time and experience to get things right but you'll eventually figure out how to streamline the photoshoot process.

Title

Most of the listing details are self-explanatory. The two main sections however, are your title and the description. The title is the main way for buyers to find your listing. Like other shopping sites, Etsy is a search engine.

That means that you have to pay attention to search engine optimization (SEO) to help to ensure that your listings appear, preferably at the top of the search results. All this may sound too techy for some but in a nutshell, high search rankings give your listings *visibility*. People are not going to buy unless they first see your awesome item.

I'll admit that because companies keep their search engine algorithms a secret, SEO requires a bit of witchery. There are however, some tricks that you can use. Firstly, you want to try to add as many popular but relevant keyword search terms into your title. A trick to find popular Etsy search terms is to start typing into the search box.

Let's say you're selling pillows. To find the most popular search terms, slowly type in your word. Etsy will then pull up the most popular search terms based on what you've typed in so far. This will not only give an idea of what to put in your title, but may also give you ideas for future product development based on market searches.

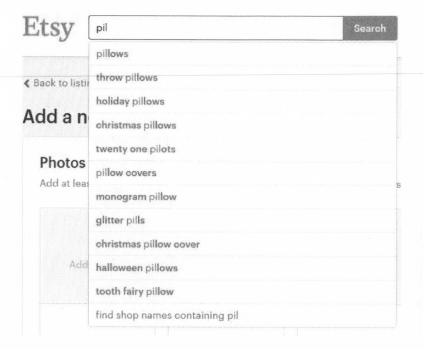

Other places to look for keywords include Google AdWords (http://google.com/adwords), Google Analytics (http://www.google.com/analytics) and MerchantWords (http://merchantwords.com).

MerchantWords is a paid subscription service (at $30/month, it is not cheap) but you can search up to 5 keywords a day for free. The site will then pull up the main keyword searches on Amazon US. Amazon is a bit of a different beast than Etsy but the search results may still offer some insights There are more functions that come with the paid subscription but if you're just starting out, I suggest just going with the free version.

Look for and use a mix of short-tail (generic) keywords like "pillow" or "throw pillow" with long-tail keywords that are more specific like "green tooth fairy throw pillow". While the short-tail words will bring in more traffic, the long-tail words are actually better because they bring in better, more qualified traffic from people who are looking for something that you are specifically selling. These people are usually more ready to buy as well.

Etsy allows you to add up to 140 characters (which includes spaces) in the title, so make full use of them. Void references to price or shipping. Etsy is not eBay or Amazon. People are on Etsy to look for something unique. Something of quality. References to low pricing undermines that. Don't use all caps or waste characters by adding words like "wow" or using special characters like "!" or "?" unless it's relevant.

Good terms to include would be the materials (eg 18K gold, organic cotton, maple etc), who it is for (teen guys, baby girl, soccer moms etc), size (L, XXL, XS etc), color (navy blue, turquoise, rainbow etc), how it's made (handwoven, wildcrafted etc), period (vintage, retro, 1940s etc), style (victorian, goth, pacific northwest, dutch etc) and smells (chocolate, fall, pumpkin spice etc).

While the title should be keyword-rich, it should also make sense to a human reader. The most important keywords should ideally be in the front of the title to maximize the search importance. For example, "18K White Gold Handmade Victorian-Inspired Dainty Custom Mom Earrings w/ Natural Red Ruby & Yellow Diamond Gemstone Pretty Gift Box for Mother's Birthday" took 139 characters and was stuffed with keywords but still makes sense to a human reader. If you're making references to seasons like Valentine's Day, Christmas or spring, make sure that you update your titles when the season passes

Description

Your item description is where you help to really reel your customer in. Note that the "description" is not just a description where you say something like "a lovely handwoven shawl, 36 inches long. Available in green or white."

Rather, the description should include copy. Copy is writing whose purpose is to *sell*. Like photography, copywriting is a skill that needs to be developed. Generally, you want to get sell the benefits (not the functions) of your product to your buyer.

A short, well-written description that is quick to skim through, followed by bullet points help to keep things neat and draw the important points. Include a short call to action at the end. An example would be:

Surprise mom with gorgeous handcrafted gold earrings that dangle down to the jawline. Comes in your choice of 18K white or yellow gold as well as 4 different gemstone options. Packaged ready for gift-giving, these are sure to please her!

Gemstone Options:
- *Natural Rubies*
- *Natural Sapphires*
- *Natural Emeralds*
- *Natural Tanzanites*

Note also, that Etsy will use the first 160 characters of your item description to create the meta description for your listing page. This is important because it is the description that will be show in search engine results as text under the main search hit.

Full Description example:

Looking for something simple and elegant but unique for your sophisticated mom? These carefully handcrafted 18K gold earrings are sure to please her for any special occasion. You choose the gemstones -- birthstones are a favorite choice for many!

Why spend anymore time shopping retail outlets when this perfect gift will be carefully packed and shipped in a gift-worthy box and delivered right to your mom with a few clicks of the button? Order these earrings today and make your mom one happy lady.

You may also include a backstory about the item or what inspired you to make the item. Maybe you're traveling the world and you found some very unusual beads that only one Nepalese woman makes, or your daughter has skin that's very sensitive to commercial soaps so you came up with your own recipe that doesn't bother her skin. Adding a human element to your brand can help to boost sales.

Again, bullet points work well in the description. Other good points to follow when crafting your descriptions:

1. Be sure to use complete sentences and correct spelling and grammar.
2. Organize information in paragraphs with similar information grouped together.
3. Include specific information like size, shape, color, age, manufacture date, country of origin, company/artist/author, and notable features or markings.
4. Clearly state the item's condition, such as new (for supplies), vintage, new old-stock or handmade. Be sure to mention any flaws.
5. Be clear about what's included and the type of packaging. Photographs of gift-worthy packaging are helpful.

6. Make the description as readable as possible.
7. Don't say anything that isn't true.
8. Don't include negative comments.
9. Don't include fine print which buyers may not read.

The full description will help to close the deal after you've reeled the customer in with your description summary. Here, you want to try to hit as many relevant keywords in your copy as possible. It shouldn't, however, be stuffed with the same term or keyword density, otherwise Google will assume that you're keyword spamming.

To keep on Google's good side, aim to use the same terms about 1-2% of the entire copy. This is called the keyword density. So, for example, you don't want to say, "this stunning dress will look great" eight times in your text. Change it up a bit. Varying words will also give you a chance to hit more potentially good keywords.

If your text is already published, you can use networkmarketingninjas.com (http://hyperurl.co/keyworddensity) to check the keyword density. If your copy has not been published, you can use SEOBook (http://hyperurl.co/seokeyword) to test your text. Keep tweaking your copy. Nothing is set in stone and that you can always revise your description.

Shop Sections

Below the description text box is an option to add sections. I highly recommend adding sections not only to keep your shop easier to navigate, but to again help to boost your SEO. Each section has its own landing page with a page title based on the named section. These specific links also come in handy when you want to market specific items according to category or theme.

Search engines will crawl each section page and show about 66 characters for each page hit but Etsy limits section names to 24 characters. Keep the section names short and sweet. Ideas with which to curate sections can include use (bracelets, rings, earrings etc), age range, color, material, production method (knitted, woven, crocheted etc), country of origin (for supplies).

You can edit shop section listings after they go live by going to *Your shop > Quick links > Listings Manager*. There should be a button labeled "Sections" in the left toolbar and click **Manage** to edit them.

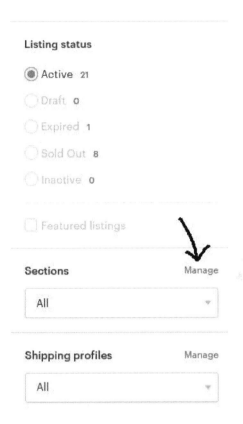

Pricing

Figuring out your pricing can be a little bit of a conundrum. It's important not to undersell yourself and your products because a low price doesn't always translate to more sales. In many cases, customers equate low prices to low quality. This isn't the race to the bottom. Many buyers are willing to pay for quality, personalization and uniqueness. More importantly, you have to make sure that you keep your business profitable. Otherwise, you won't be in business very long.

Even though most people starting out won't have overheads like warehousing and employees, you'll still have to factor in your material costs, costs to obtain and/or use supplies, tools, equipment and packing materials. There are also transaction fees which include Etsy fees ($0.20 fee per listing + 3.5% on final sales price) and Paypal/Etsy Direct Checkout transaction fees (which vary around $0.25 + 3.5% per transaction).

In terms of markups, I personally won't go less than a 100% markup on materials. This helps me to cover the costs and time involved in getting said supplies while still making some money. Next figure out the time (in hours) you spend making your products and multiply the number of hours by an hourly wage rate that is fair to you. Packing and shipping can take up considerable time so factor this in as well.

In the beginning, you'll probably need more time to both make and pack your orders. In time, the process should take less time as you learn to work faster and to streamline your processes better. Once you've figured out your pricing structure, investigate the pricing model of 5 or more shops which sell items that are similar to yours, and that are selling. Depending on the shop's size and number of items on sale, a good sales gauge number is about 50 sales per month.

It is very easy to see the number of sales a shop has made since its Etsy inception. On the shop's main page, Etsy will list the shop's location, the number of total sales made since its inception, and the year the shop was started. Divide the number of sales by the approximate number of months since the shop opened. Etsy may change its layout and interface over time but the idea remains the same.

In the example below, this shop has sold 1326 items since 2013 (3 years ago). 1326/36 months equals about 36 sales/month. Not a bad shop to emulate.

Note that this comparison method may only give you part of the picture. For example, I make most of my sales on my own website and use Etsy only as a sales outpost. The shop's pricing will also vary depending on product quality and uniqueness.

For example, let's say you're selling gold jewelry and you've found a shop that sells comparable designs that sell well. You can bounce off their pricing structure but if you're selling 14K gold jewelry as compared to their 18-24K gold, you'll need to factor the quality difference into your pricing structure as well.

As a general rule, I would price a product line a little bit less than the most expensive successful shop's prices. That way, you don't lose the image of brand quality but your brand is still a little bit more affordable than the most expensive brands. I say this generally because it all boils down to your brand. My product is all about value and affordability. Pricing it above similar products will go against the idea of why we developed it in the first place.

If you're making something of really high quality, then maybe you should price higher than most. Keep your target audience in mind. For example, the single, high-powered executive will probably have more disposable income than say, the stay-at-home suburban mom with three young children. If your product is aimed at the former, you can generally get away with charging more. Just remember that you don't want to price your products out of the market either.

Set your prices to end with a "99" rather than a whole number (for example, charge $12.99 rather than $13 or $12.50). There is a reason why some big retailers price in this manner - people have been conditioned to think that prices ending in "99" indicate a deal or a discount point, even if that's not necessarily true. A study by M.I.T.'s Sloan School of Management found that they "were able to increase demand by a third by raising the price of a dress from $34 to $39. By comparison, changing the price from $34 to $44 yielded no difference in demand."

Regardless, always keep your time and material cost in mind. Remember, we're working towards building a sustainably profitable business. Keep testing and tweaking price-points. It may actually be more profitable to charge a little less, and sell more items that require a lot less cost and labor (eg selling prints or supplies) than trying to sell a lot of high-priced, one-of-a-kind large paintings where the market will be much smaller.

Payment Methods

Etsy allows sellers to accept a number of payment methods including: credit or debit cards, Etsy gift cards, Apple Pay, iDeal (from buyers in Netherlands), Sofort (from buyers in Austria and Germany) and Paypal. The nice thing about Etsy is that they have now integrated Paypal payments into Direct Checkout. That means you can still accept Paypal even if you don't have a Paypal account.

The funds are swept into your Etsy deposit account and are then direct-deposited into your bank account at scheduled intervals. If you live in a country that is not supported by Direct Checkout, you can still accept payments via Paypal directly. You can refer to Etsy's list of countries that are eligible for Direct Checkout at http://hyperurl.co/etsycountries.

If you choose *Enable manual payment methods*, you can also opt to accept checks and/or money orders by mail. You may also opt to accept other payment options like bitcoin, that are not currently supported by Etsy.

Include all the necessary payment information as well as payment terms, deadlines for payment receipt, shop policies etc. Try to be as clear as possible to avoid misunderstandings and use Conversations or "Convo", Etsy's online messaging system to contact your buyer as soon as possible.

If your shop isn't yet open, you can choose or revise payment options under the "Get Paid" tab after you've chosen your shop name and listed an item. If your shop is open to the public, you can choose your payment options by clicking *Your shop > Finances > Accepted payments* (http://hyperurl.co/etsypayments).

Packing & Shipping

Etsy allows you to charge for shipping in three ways: free shipping, flat shipping charges (meaning everyone pays the same charge, regardless of shipping distance, which can affect postage rates) and calculated shipping charges.

Unless you're selling very large or heavy items that can justify high shipping charges, or you're shipping overseas (where postage charge can add up quickly), resist the urge to try charging an unreasonably high flat rate shipping charge. Buyers are not dumb. If they think they will be fleeced in shipping charges, they simply will not buy from you. If you have a very good reason for an unusually high charge, state that reason clearly in your description.

I recommend that you use Etsy's calculated shipping charges to figure out the shipping price based on your package's weight and size. In the **Shipping section** of the selling form, select **Calculate them for me** in the drop down menu. Enter your shipping **origination zip code**.

Processing & Handling Time

Next, enter your **Processing (handling) time**. This should include the entire order turnaround time, from the time the buyer orders to the time the package is dropped off in the mail.

That means you have to include your processing time, especially if you're making-to-order on a part-time basis. Give yourself a few extra days leeway in case you get swamped or other issues crop up. Include the time it will take for you to pack and ship as well. If you are starting out, do not burn yourself out. Give yourself about 3 business days to ship (not including time to make) items.

Business days do not include postal holidays. Do not waste time and gas to ship one or two items everyday! This lag time allows you to collect your orders together to make a combined postal drop off at the post office. It does not make sense to have to go to the post office everyday to ship an item.

If you have a standalone mailbox and if your packages are small enough to fit in it, you can leave your shipments in the mailbox for pickup. Collect mail from the day before, place the items you need shipped out, shut the mailbox and flip the little red flag on the right side of the mailbox up. The flag will indicate to the mail carrier that there is outgoing mail.

When you expand your business, consider investing in the largest mailbox available so that you can place more outgoing mail in it. This will save you trips to the post office. Buyers are more likely to buy if you ship quickly but understand, that many Etsy sellers need time to make their orders.

Shipping Destinations

Next, choose the **shipping destinations** that you will ship to. You can choose to ship only domestically, which removes some of the problems of shipping overseas, like dealing with added shipping time frames, shipping logistics and international customs.

However, you also shut out a potentially large market for your products if you only choose to only ship domestically. If you're starting out, you might want to choose to only ship domestically until you get your feet a little wet.

Shipping Service Options

Etsy allows you to offer a range of USPS shipping options where it will automatically calculate the charges based on your package details and buyer location. I recommend offering at least both USPS First Class shipping (for packages 13 oz and under) and USPS Priority Mail options. You can also offer USPS Express Mail or USPS Parcel Ground (for packages over 13 oz).

It takes time and some experience to figure out packaging logistics so if you feel uncomfortable with packing and shipping, consider starting by shipping everything via USPS Priority Mail. Priority Mail costs more than regular mail but the USPS will provide you with free boxes and packing tape. Priority Mail boxes come in a multitude of sizes so you should be able to find one to meet your needs. You will still need to supply your own cushioning materials.

As long as you have at least one Priority Mail or Express package, you can have the USPS pick your entire shipment for the day at the location of your choosing (eg front door, back door, porch etc). You can even put a note in your pickup request to tell the USPS where you need your items picked up when the mailman comes around. If you are unable to leave your packages unattended, you can request the mail carrier to knock on your door for pickup. Schedule pickups at http://1.usa.gov/1kNi08k.

Branded Packaging

Etsy is one place where branding is particularly important. You want to try to turn that one-time customer into a repeat customer, so you want them to recognize you! Use a cohesive design and/or color scheme to keep your brand recognizable. You also want to use packaging materials that are in keeping with your target audience and brand image.

For example, I use very simple packaging, right down to hand-writing most of my address labels. My packing style aligns with my store product and brand story -- no frills, affordable, mom & pop- made product. If you're selling high-priced items for the sophisticated lady, it would probably be a good to avoid using any kind of obviously recycled packaging.

Some simple techniques to brand your shipments include adding a removable a sticker with your shop name or logo on the back or base of the products (make sure that the sticker can be removed without damaging the product itself.

You can also make hang tags. These add a professional but homey touch, especially if they are handmade. You can make hang tags yourself or buy them on Etsy. As you become more established, you might want to order a custom stamp. These aren't very expensive. I often find additional discount deals from discount sites like Groupon (http://groupon.com).

You can use wrapping techniques that do not have to be costly to look nice. If done right, simple materials like organza, burlap, twine, ribbons, lace, washi tape, brown paper and even newspaper or paper from phonebooks can add pazazz to the final product. Adding photos of your packaged products can also help to seal the deal.

Finally, it is also a good idea to add a business card to every order. Many shop owners include a discount code for future purchases to draw customers back. Again, you can order custom business cards quite affordably from websites like Vistaprint (http://vistaprint.com).

If you want business cards with a more luxurious feel, Moo (http://moo.com) is a little more costly but they make very nice ones. You can even order "series packs" which feature different images on different cards. This option offers a bit of a "wow" factor while featuring more than one of your products.

Outer Packaging

Small items can be packed in regular envelopes, bubble envelopes or in the case of posters, tubes. Larger or heavy items will need to be shipped in a box but where possible, I try to avoid having to buy shipping boxes. What kind of boxes do you look for? Use boxes with firm, corrugated cardboard.

Do not use flimsy one-layer cardboard. Also make sure that the cardboard used to make the boxes is not too thick unless you need to package heavy items. Sturdy, thick cardboard boxes will add a lot of weight to your shipment and drive your shipping costs up.

The kind of boxes that Amazon uses to ship their items in is the ideal cardboard thickness for shipping most items. USPS Priority Mail boxes are also made from cardboard of suitable thickness. I often reuse Amazon boxes but if you want to keep your branding more neutral, you should be able to get free boxes of all shapes and sizes at big box craft stores like Hobby Lobby, or smaller grocery stores (I have never approached big box grocers like Walmart but I have not had problems approaching the staff at my local Safeway). Choose only clean, undamaged boxes and boxes that have not been water damaged. Water-damaged boxes may not be strong enough to withstand the rigors of shipment.

Do not use boxes that are too small or unnecessarily big. Oversized boxes add too much weight to your package and makes your item more susceptible to getting damaged because the item tends to roll around more in a large package. Using a box that is too small will not provide adequate space to properly cushion your item. Use bubble wrap or air packs as shown and cushion all sides of your item.

You can also use clean, empty paper-based egg cartons or balled up newspaper as cushioning but it will add more weight to your package. Do not use stiff and/or glossy magazine paper which is heavy and ineffective. Do not use styrofoam packing peanuts. They are hard to handle and do not protect items properly. Items jostle way to much within the peanuts.

If you are concerned about how using recycled shipping materials may look to your customer, simply put this notice in all your auctions: "To help reduce environmental waste, and to help you save on shipping costs, please understand that I use recycled packing materials. My recycling helps keep prices lower for my buyers." Again, using this option may or may not be appropriate, depending on your brand and customer demographics.

Items like plush toys or clothes that will not get crushed can be shipped in appropriately sized manila envelopes or plastic-bag mailers. Flat, easily bendable items like postcards or trading cards are best shipped sandwiched between sturdy cardboard with an outer cardboard margin of at least half an inch all around which will help protect the sides and corners from getting dented or damaged during shipment. Use cardboard similar in thickness to the USPS Priority Mail cardboard box thickness. You cannot use Priority Mail supplies for non-Priority Mail shipments. Posters are best shipped rolled up in a tube.

Use good quality packing tape to tape all your packages. You do not need your packing tape failing on you during transit! Places to find mailing supplies include your expected places like eBay, Amazon, Walmart, Staples as well as uline.com, upaknship.com, packagingsupplies.com, papermart.com, royalmailers.com and associatedbag.com.

Handling Fees

Next, you can add a handling fee that will be tagged on to the actual shipping charges. As a customer, I used to think handling fees were a ripoff. That was until I became a seller. In addition to packaging costs, packing and shipping takes a lot of *time*.

As with flat-rate shipping charges, avoid the urge to charge too much. A $1-$5 handling charge is usually fair unless your package needs very special handling. Shipping furniture, for example would be one of those instances where your handling costs will be significantly higher.

Package Dimensions & Weight

Finally, you'll need to enter your package's weight and shipping dimensions. To determine your package's weight, weigh the item plus all the packing and cushioning material plus the box you plan to ship it in. This is where having a digital scale comes in handy. However, you can also get it weighed at the post office.

Do *not* assume or estimate a package's weight or dimensions! Some items, especially some cloth or paper-based products can look deceptively light but end up actually being quite heavy. Mis-estimation of shipping weight and/or size can be a costly mistake that turns your profit into a loss.

If you have added preset shipping information, Etsy will automatically calculate the shipping charge to the buyer based on the package weight and size, current USPS rates and the package's destination. The automatic calculation is handy, especially since it saves you the trouble of having to recalculate your shipping charges when shipping carriers increase their rates.

If you're selling similar or variations of the same item, it'll be a good idea to save the shipping profile.

Once saved, Etsy will have that saved shipping profile ready for use if applicable.

A note on free shipping: I don't think it's necessary to offer free shipping. It's not a common practice on Etsy and saves you the hassle of having to refigure your sales price to factor in postage increases.

Search Terms

While Etsy lists the **Search terms** section as optional, you really should add in the tag information. The tag can consist of a word or a short phrase (like "crocheted pillow"). It should be relevant and accurate. Do not keyword spam the tags with irrelevant search terms.

Is is a good idea to repeat the title search terms in the tags as well. According to Etsy, *exact phrase matches are stronger than matches on individual words. For example, a search for "banana backpack" would return all items with the words "banana" and "backpack" in the tags or title, but items with "banana backpack" in the title would be considered a closer match.*

If a word or phrase in a buyer's search appears in both the title and tags of a listing, the search algorithm considers that listing more relevant than a listing with that word or phrase in the tags or title alone.

Etsy allows you to use up to 13 tags so the more you add, the better your chance of the item been seen in searches.

Shop Policy

Post Sale Information

Be clear with post-sale information. Include care information, clarity on any possible extra fees, taxes or charges, shipping expectations and your return policy. If you're shipping abroad, the destination country may impose an import tax on the shipment, based on the stated price on the customs form.

Since I do not know the tax rates or nuances of the international countries I ship to, I add a note stating that shipments overseas may be subject to import or customs taxes at the destination country. Buyers should check with their respective authorities to find out what those charges will be.

Be realistic with turnaround times and shipping timelines based on your schedule as well as the season. For many shops, the period before Christmas is usually the busiest time of the year. This is also the time when the Post Office is very busy so make sure that your buyers understand that shipments may take longer than usual to arrive. On the other hand, if you're selling bikinis, spring-summer may be your busiest season so advise your customers accordingly.

Return & Exchange Policy

Etsy allows you to set your own return and exchange policy. Refund options you can offer include money back only, money back or replacement (buyer choice), money back or exchange (buyer choice). Standard return policies require the buyer to return the item before they receive their refund/exchange. You will also need to specify whether you or the buyer will pay return shipping charges.

Often, custom, perishable, used, damaged or soil and/or digital orders are not eligible for return or exchange unless there is an error on your part. If you choose to accept returns, a 14 or 30 day return window is reasonable. 60 day-returns is generous. I offer a no-time-limit, no questions asked return policy.

However, I sell a low-cost item and our return-rates are low. If I were selling expensive custom artwork, my return policy would be different. Set your Return Policy based on your comfort level and remember to price your products to account for costs to process the percentage of returns that you might expect to get.

According to a 2013 article on internetretailer.com, returns as a percent of total sales for online merchants is an average of about 3.5%. If you're seeing a return rate that's considerably higher, access the problem(s) and work towards eliminating them before the returns happen.

Add your return/exchange policy information to your Shop policies at: *Your shop > Edit shop* (https://www.etsy.com/shop/me/edit) and scroll down to *Shop policies.*

About Section

Etsy is very much about marketplace and customer experience. Completing the **About section** will not only help to create more brand awareness for you, but Etsy will also reward you by giving your shop a better search placement if you have completed this section. That means that your items will show up higher in searches if you've completed the **About, Policies and Shop** sections.

Again, this is another opportunity for you to convince your buyer why your product is more beneficial than other similar products. Other good information to include here may be a little bit about yourself and how your shop came about. Something like, "Since I was a child, looking up at the clouds in the sky always transported me to many imaginary worlds. Today, I hope that my cloud-themed paintings can also bring some of that childhood wonderment into your home!"

Describe how you make the goods or where you find your supplies. Do you travel the world, looking for those handmade jewelry supplies that make your accessories very unique while giving village women the opportunity to earn an income? Did you start sewing cloth diapers because you weren't able to find anything on the market that suited your needs or that of your baby's? Help the reader understand where you and your passion comes from.

Avoid adding sales pitches (a big turn off), writing super-long boring bios or anything negative like, "I hate my job and I'm hoping to be able to quit it if my Etsy business takes off." Always use an upbeat tone. Talking about adversity is fine but there should always be a positive spin or resolution to it.

Finally, always think about your customer. They want to know that they will be taken care of so make that message clear. A sincere and heartfelt story may even garner some loyal customers and fans!

Completing Your Shopfront

Just as you would think twice about stepping into a store without proper displays and signage, customers will think twice about shopping from web stores without a proper banner (your virtual store sign). Etsy allows you to add a shop banner, as well as two images: one to represent your shop and one to represent you.

The following image is Etsy's current setup. It has changed over time and will likely change again in the future but the idea remains the same.

Add or edit your shop at *Your shop > Shop settings > Info and appearance* (https://www.etsy.com/shop/me/edit).

Shop Cover Photo & Banner

The shop cover photo is your largest branding opportunity for your shop. It will appear on both desktop and mobile devices. At the time of writing, the ideal size for your cover photo is 3360 x 840 pixels and the minimal size is 1200 x 300.

You also have the option of using the original smaller banner which is centered at the top of your shop homepage. The banner however, does not appear on mobile devices. It should be sized exactly at 750x100 pixels. For the most up-to-date image size requirements, refer to Etsy's help page at (http://hyperurl.co/etsysizes).

Try to keep the cover simple. You want it to 'wow" but not to overwhelm. The cover and banner should be branded consistently with the same fonts, color scheme and images. It should also reflect the personality of your brand.

For example, if you're selling fun, flirty floral dresses, you don't want to have a store cover and banner that uses a dark color scheme and business-like models in suits. Some ideas to use for your cover can be a fun pattern or design emphasising your brand or your brand's theme or personality. It could also showcase one or a few of your product offerings. Remember: consistency is the key.

I like using Canva (http://canva.com) to set up and make my banners but you can also buy pre-made kits from many sites including from Etsy sellers. These are usually quite reasonably priced at around $20-$30. Just search for "Etsy banner sets" or use a similar search term.

If you have a larger budget, you can order more expensive sets which include branded business cards, social media banners and possibly even a website. 99designs (http://99designs.com) is one of those crowdsourced websites that offer such design services. If you're just starting out however, I recommend keeping things simpler and your startup costs down. You can always expand later you and tweak or revise your branding over time.

Profile Photo

Your profile photo needs to be 400 x 400 pixels. It should be a headshot or close-up image of yourself in good or natural lighting. Don't use photos that do not show you at your best. As you can see from the example, the profile photo is very small so avoid using unclear or dark images or full body shots.

Ideally, the image should also convey what you sell. If you can wear the items you sell in your profile photo, like hats or scarves, those work nicely in a profile photo. If you sell prints or paintings, you can try to include them in your photograph background.

Not all products can be clearly depicted in the profile photo. Sometimes, you'll have to work with the theme instead. For me, I added pictures of poultry in front of me. If you sell outdoor wear, you might want to be photographed outdoors. If you sew, you can picture yourself with a sewing tape measure draped on your neck. These ideas won't apply to everyone but do the best you can where applicable.

Shop Icon or Image

Your shop icon needs to be 500 x 500 pixels. It should look good big or small and reflect your shop's brand and personality. It can be a logo or an image that represents your shop or your products. Keep logos, graphics or illustrations simple.

If you're using text, make it short and easy to read. Don't use long words, a lot of text or busy backgrounds that take away from the image or that make things hard to read.

If you want a logo and aren't able to come up with one yourself, good places to hire a freelancer include Fiverr (http://fiverr.com), UpWork (http://upwork.com), Etsy itself and again on the higher end, 99designs.

If you have some time and creativity, you can also create logos for free at Logogarden (http://logogarden.com), Logotypemaker.com and my favorite site, Canva (http://canva.com). There are many free or low cost logo generators online if you Google for them. Just be sure to read the fine print of these sites before you start because many of these "free" sites will charge for large, high resolution downloads.

Another alternative is to use free images or clipart to make your logo. Do not just use any image you find online. Most are copyrighted. You can buy stock images from websites like Shutterstock (http://shutterstock) or Dreamstime (http://dreamstime), which I've used before and liked for their fair prices. Just make sure that you're in compliance with their image licensing use.

Always save your licensing paperwork in case there are disputes in the future. Alternatively, you can also use public domain images. My personal favorite site to find public domain images is pixabay (http://pixabay.com). Add some text and you've made yourself a logo!

Adobe Photoshop or Illustrator are good for putting your logo together but have an expense and learning curve to them. For free options, again, I like Canva (http://canva.com) or Gimp (http://gimp.com), which is a free downloadable software.

If you're using photo editors that allow you upload fonts, again, make sure that the fonts you're using can be used for commercial purposes representing your business. To sidestep this issue, I use Google Fonts (http://fonts.google.com).

You can also use a more unique font to make a logo and skip the images! In fact, you really don't need fancy fonts or images to make your logo. Think about Google's, Amazon's, Target's, Etsy's and just about any big company's logo and you'll notice that they're all very simple. It is more important that your business is always branded appropriately, consistently and memorably.

Customer Service

Now that you are officially in business, you have to provide customer service. Even if you are selling items part-time or as a hobby, you must maintain good to excellent customer service. When a customer asks you a question through Etsy (called "Convo"), Etsy will forward the question to the email you have on file. Do not respond directly to Etsy's email. Instead, you need to reply using the "Respond" button in the email, which will take you back to Etsy's convo message system on Etsy.

Respond honestly and as quickly as possible to customer questions or queries. Make sure that you understand what is being asked before answering. If it is not clear, email the customer back for a clarification. Many people want to buy quickly. If they have to wait too long for your answer, they may move on to the next seller.

If you are unable to check your Etsy correspondence often because of other commitments like a job or kids etc, set aside a fixed time slot where you can commit to your Etsying. This can be before work or lunchtime, or whatever works for you. Put a note in your shop policies or FAQs or the description itself to let your customers know that this is the time that you are able to communicate with them. Something like:

"I take my Etsy customers and business seriously. However, at this time, I can only sell on Etsy part-time (although I hope to become full-time with

your business!) I am unable to Etsy while at work. I am only able to answer emails during [time]-[time] [time zone] on weekdays and [time][time zone] on weekends. Thank you so much for your patience and understanding! :)"

Do the same thing if you have health issues or any other issues that may affect your customer service and/or handling times. Including a smiley face in all your responses helps keep communication more friendly. I have found that people are more understanding if you are upfront with them on what to expect *before* they deal with you.

Poor customer service like slow communication or lack of communication, poor (rude) communication, too many items getting damaged in shipping without resolution or taking a lot longer to ship that the stated handling time are all examples of poor customer service. Poor customer service can not only ruin a seller's reputation, too many complaints can result in Etsy giving your items lower visibility or worse - a selling suspension. Suspensions may be temporary or permanent.

Marketing

Unfortunately, in this crowded marketplace, your business is no longer the case of "if you build it, they will come." While it is a very good idea to follow the tips and tricks covered in previous chapters to get better search visibility, it may not be necessarily enough.

There are a great number of marketing tactics including advertising on Facebook, Pinterest and Instagram to name a few outlets. Even if you're not ready to advertise or become active on any or all of these platforms, is a good idea to at least register your brand on the main social media websites: Facebook, Twitter, Pinterest, Instagram and possibly, LinkedIn (if your target audience is business women).

Again, keep things consistent. You don't have to be everywhere at once or necessarily everywhere but it helps to at least have your foot in the door when you're ready to spread your wings. Because one could write a book or books on the how-tos of each platform, I'll just focus on some more Etsy-specific marketing options.

Make Connections

Unlike other selling platforms like eBay and Amazon, Etsy is concentrated on fostering a strong community between buyers, sellers and its employees. Being active in the community still help you get noticed by sellers and buyers alike because each influences the other.

Making connections can be as simple as adding favorites or "hearts" to the items you like and making your own curated lists. Every time you do that, the seller is informed of your action. If your lists are made public, it gives that seller a chance at more visibility. The same applies to your items and brand when someone favorites your item or shop.

Each connection you make gives you an opportunity to get mentioned or featured in someone's curated list, in a review or blog post. This in turn, can help to increase awareness to your brand and increase sales.

Etsy Teams

Teams (https://www.etsy.com/teams) are a group of sellers with something in common. The commonality may be based on what the sellers sell (like only kitchen tools) or by location (eg all the team members live in East Texas).

Both kinds of teams are good ways for you to form mutually beneficial relationships with other sellers. The teams you're in are featured on your Etsy profile so buyers are exposed to a range of shops that may be more relevant to their taste and interests.

Being a part of these teams can also translate because it makes it easier to coordinate co-benefi sharing a flea market booth or having a nun renting a section at a convention. You might even be able to pool resources to hire professional PR people to help to publicize your businesses or niche. Be helpful without expecting reciprocation. People will remember you and you'll find that it pays back in the long run.

Tastemakers

Etsy Tastemakers (https://www.etsy.com/pages) usually have an affiliation to an established brand. The brand may be associated with a media publication, retail enterprise or an academic or work organization. Like most others, these Tastemakers have affinities to certain products or themes and curate items from other sellers that help to build an extension of their own brand.

Try to have your products fit into as many curated lists as you can. Here's how:

1. Review the list of Tastemakers and do some background research on any Tastemaker that has a list that matches with your products or brand. Add all of them to your narrowed list of Tastemakers.
2. Be helpful. Promote their brand or lists on your Etsy page, in social media, in articles or blog posts or

however other way you can think of to help someone else. Send them the link to that article.

3. Contact the Tastemaker with your admiration for their lists and suggest your item that would make a good candidate for one of their lists. Include some information about your brand/story, your product and some photos for them to consider.

4. If you want to really make an impression, send them a sample of your product.

Expect to hear some "nos" and help without expecting anything in return. Not every Tastemaker will reciprocate the same way. Some, especially big brands, may not even respond but keep trying. Tastemakers can affect which shops customers patronage and what they buy so it is worth putting in the effort to try to establish a contact with them.

Etsy Ads

Etsy Ads is another way for your to get more visibility for your items. It is basically a pay-per-click format where you bid on a certain maximum price that you're willing to pay for your ad to appear on top or higher in the listings when that term is searched.

You can enter a manual bid for each search term, or you can let Etsy bid automatically for you. The minimum daily advertising budget is $1 while the maximum is $10. The plus side to a manually-set bid price is that you can set the price you're willing to pay per click.

However, if you set it too low in relation to others' bids, your ad will not be served. Choosing the automatic bidding is more streamlined, especially if you want your ad to keep serving. Unfortunately, if you don't keep tabs on it, bids can get quite expensive at over $0.50 per click. If those clicks don't convert, you can lose money quickly.

I've had both good and bad experiences with Etsy Ads. As long as the click-price is fairly low (about $0.12 for me) and conversion (that is number of clicks divided by number of sales) is decent, I make decent profit. If it goes higher, I start losing money. Advertising during my product's off-season has also not been cost-effective for me. The important thing it to keep an eye on conversations and keep tweaking your search terms. Visit *Your shop* > *Promote* > *Advertising dashboard* (https://www.etsy.com/advertising) to try your hand at it.

Google Shopping Ads

Google Shopping Ads that Etsy recently launched functions in a way that's similar to Etsy ads except that in this case, instead of your listings getting visibility from Etsy browsers, your listings will be shown in Google searches.

Etsy used to sponsor Google shopping ads but it is now a separate service that you have to pay for. Again, you can have a minimum budget of $1/day and a maximum of $10/day but you don't have to bid on individual search terms. Etsy will sync with Google to show your listings if your bids fit the advertising range.

At this time, I won't spend extra to advertise on Google shopping ads because based on my shop stats, I haven't had a great deal of traffic to Etsy from Google. I also don't know the conversation rates per click. I therefore don't want to commit too much advertising money to driving buyers to my Etsy storefront, especially since Etsy is only a small branch of my business.

Coupons

Finally, Etsy allows you to offer coupons for sales events. There are three kinds of coupons: discounts off a fixed dollar amount with a minimum dollar-spend, a percent-off discount or free shipping coupons. These coupons are good when you're contacting bloggers for a product review or running a social media promotion as it lowers to barrier for customers to buy your items.

Keeping Track of Your Sales

It is a good idea to keep track of your sales. You can use a notebook or Microsoft Excel if you have it. If you do not, you can use Open Office (http://www.openoffice.org/) which is free, or Google Docs/Google Drive (https://drive.google.com/). I like Google Drive best because everything is automatically saved on a Cloud and I no longer have to worry about losing my records if my computer fails me.

Things to keep track of include inventory costs, shipping costs, mailing supply costs, mileage, overhead expenses (internet costs, electricity etc), equipment (computers, printers etc) costs, fees and commissions etc.

You can keep track of your sales revenue at *Your shop > Quick links > Stats* (https://www.etsy.com/your/shops/me/stats). There, you can also review traffic sources as well as top keywords and your shop's most active items.

Keep all your receipts as well as records of your mileage etc (if applicable). I am old-fashioned and just keep all my receipts in an accordion folder. I record my mileage in a notebook that I keep in my car. Once taxes are done, I move all my receipts to a box for that tax year and start the receipt storage for the new tax year.

These are just examples of what I do. This should not be construed as tax, financial or any other professional

advice. **Please consult a tax or financial professional to help you figure out what works for you!**

Etsy Pattern Store

Etsy recently launched their Pattern subscription service, which basically allows you to turn your Etsy shop into your own "custom" shop. My suggestion is to avoid this service. It is still part of Etsy and you do not really own the shop. Rather, it is just a mirror of your Etsy storefront with a custom URL which appears as though it's not running as part of Etsy, even though it is. Search engines do not like mirrored sites and will lower your search ranking, reducing site search visibility.

The two main problems I see are that you're still digital sharecropping on Etsy's platform. If, for some reason they decide to suspend your account, you're out of luck if they don't reinstate you. This has happened to sellers before, sometimes for reasons unknown to the seller.

If you're working on building your own brand, I recommend building your own store separate from any selling platform. Moreover, I think that the monthly subscription fee of $15 is very high for what little you get out of the deal.

If you're starting out but want to build your brand from the get-go, a better alternative would be to register your own domain name. There are many name registrars including GoDaddy.com and Namecheap.com but the cheapest registrar that I've found is NameSilo.com, which charges a flat $8/year.

You can then forward your URL to point to your Etsy storefront.

Branching Away from Etsy

As your business and brand grows, instead of subscribing to Etsy Pattern, set up your own storefront. Most are also cheaper than using Etsy's Pattern subscription rates. These days, there are many options including (in alphabetical order) but not limited to:

1. BigCommerce.com
2. Freewebstore.com
3. Shopify.com
4. Squarespace.com
5. Weebly.com
6. Wix.com
7. Wordpress.org
8. WooCommerce.com

Many people like using Wordpress with plugins but to be honest, I couldn't figure out how to make it work. I currently use Wix and like it for its easy customization, drag-and-drop elements, nice interface. Other services may either cost more or offer less customization abilities. However, they may have more or better functions that are more suited to your needs.

Even though many of these sites offer the option of registering your domain for you as part of the subscription fee, it is a good idea to register your domain with a separate domain registrar. In the event that something happens to the web hosting company, be it the company going out of business or you wanting to move your site to different host for another reason, you will still be able to point your URL to a new storefront.

Conclusion

Let your business grow and evolve with you. Don't let your vision guide you solely. Paying attention to what your customers are looking for can help to propel your brand to new and greater heights.

As you get bigger, continue to utilize Etsy's brand and marketing machine to help grow your business. Look into partnership opportunities with Etsy Wholesale, which in the past, have included partnership opportunities with Whole Foods and The Minneapolis Institute of Art.

Keep using Etsy to help you grow but also look into developing your own wings by opening your own storefront once you take flight. I wish you the best of luck in your journey!

Sign up for my newsletter at http://byjillb.com and get THREE e-books for free:

HOW TO KEEP BACKYARD CHICKENS
CAN DOS & DON'TS
THE MODERN AMERICAN FRUGAL HOUSEWIFE

Disclaimer and Disclosure

This guide is for entertainment and informational purposes only. The author and anyone associated with this book shall not be held liable for damages incurred through the use of information provided herein. Content included on this book is not intended to be, nor does it constitute, the giving of medical or professional advice. The author and others associated with this book make no representation as to the accuracy, completeness or validity of any information in this book.

While every caution has been taken to provide the most accurate information, please use your own discretion before making any decisions based solely on the content herein. The author and others associated with this book are not liable for any errors or omissions nor will they provide any form of compensation if you suffer an inconvenience, loss or damages of any kind because of, or by making use of, the information contained herein. Any opinion given is the author's own, based on her experience. If in doubt, always seek the advice of a professional who can advise you appropriately before acting on any part of this book.

This book contains references and links to other Third Party products and services. Some of these references have been included for the convenience of the readers and to make the book more complete. They should not be construed as endorsements from, or of, any of these Third Parties or their products or services. These links and references may contain products and opinions expressed by their respective owners. The author does not assume liability or responsibility for any Third Party material or opinions. The author is the owner of Chicken Armor® hen saddles and profits from sales at chickenarmor.com.

Resources

Business Entity Search/Registration

Knowem.com (http://knowem.com)

US Employer Identification Number

(http://1.usa.gov/1hBUiLt)

US Patent & Trademark Office (http://hyperurl.co/uspto)

Domain Registrars

GoDaddy (http://godaddy.com)

Name Cheap (http://namecheap.com)

Name Silo (http://namesilo.com)

Image/Font Resources

Dreamstime (http://dreamstime)

Google Fonts (http://fonts.google.com)

Pixabay (http://pixabay.com)

Shutterstock (http://shutterstock.com)

Keyword Research Resources

Google AdWords (http://google.com/adwords)

Google Analytics (http://www.google.com/analytics**)**

MerchantWords (http://merchantwords.com)

Keyword Density Search

Networkmarketingninjas.com

(http://hyperurl.co/keyworddensity)

SEOBook (http://hyperurl.co/seokeyword)

Logo/Banner Designers
99designs (http://99designs.com)
Canva (http://canva.com)
Fiverr (http://fiverr.com)
Logogarden (http://logogarden.com)
Logotypemaker (http://logotypemaker.com)
Upwork (http://upwork.com)

Marketing & Packing Supply Resources
Associated Bag (http://associatedbag.com)
Moo (http://moo.com)
Packagingsupplies (http://packagingsupplies.com)
PaperMart (http://papermart.com)
Royal Mailers (http://royalmailers.com)
Uline (http://uline.com)
Upaknship (http://upaknship.com)
Vistaprint (http://vistaprint.com)

Photo Editors
Adobe Photoshop/Illustrator/Lightroom (http://adobe.com)
Gimp (http://gimp.com)
PicMonkey (http://picmonkey.com)
Pixlr (http://pixlr.com)

Record-Keeping Resources
Evernote (http://evernote.com)
Pinterest (http://pinterest.com)

Webstore Resources

BigCommerce (http://bigcommerce.com)

Freewebstore (http://freewebstore.com)

Shopify (http://shopify.com)

Squarespace (http://squarespace.com)

Weebly (http://weebly.com)

Wix (http://wix.com)

Wordpress.org (http://wordpress.org)

WooCommerce (http://woocommerce.com)

References

"6 Ways to Elevate Your Photography", Taylor Combs, 2015

"Branded Packaging Basics", Katy Svehaug, 2013

"Branding 101", Dixie Laite, 2013

"Etsy Excellence", Tyco Press, 2015

Etsy Seller Help Section, Etsy.com, 2016

"The Handmade Entrepreneur", Dani Marie, 2015

Books By Jill b.

Please check out my other books at **http://byjillb.com**:

The Modern Frugal American Housewife Book #1
Home Economics

The Modern Frugal American Housewife Book #2
Organic Gardening

The Modern Frugal American Housewife Book #3
Moms Edition

The Modern Frugal American Housewife Book #4
Emergency Prepping

How to Keep Backyard Chickens
A Straightforward Beginner's Guide

The Best Backyard Chicken Breeds
A List of Top Birds for Pets, Eggs and Meat

Foraging
A Beginner's Guide to Wild Edible and Medicinal Plants

Medicinal Herb Garden
10 Plants for the Self-Reliant Homestead Prepper

Hidden
Prepper's Secret Edible Garden

CAN Dos and Don'ts
Water Bath and Pressure Canning

How to Make Money on eBay: Beginner's Guide
From Setting Up Accounts to Selling Like a Pro

How to Make Money on eBay: Maximize Profits
Secrets, Stories, Tips and Hacks - Confessions of a 16-Year eBay Veteran

How to Make Money on eBay: International Sales
Taking the Fear and Guesswork Out of Doing Business Internationally on eBay

Self-Publish on a Budget with Amazon
A Guide for the Author Publishing eBooks on Kindle

How to Start a T-Shirt Business on Merch by Amazon

How To Start An Etsy Online Business
The Creative Entrepreneur's Guide

About the Author

~ Self-Reliance: One Step at a Time ~
http://byjillb.com

Reliance on one job. Reliance on the agri-industrial food system. Are you ready to break free, take control and to rely on yourself?

With a no-nonsense style, Jill Bong draws from her own homesteading experiences and mistakes, and writes books focusing on maximizing output with minimal input to save you time and money.

Jill writes under the pen name Jill b. She is an author, entrepreneur, homesteader and is the co-inventor and co-founder of Chicken Armor® (http://chickenarmor.com), an affordable, low maintenance chicken saddle. She has also written over a dozen books on homesteading and self-reliance.

Jill has been mentioned/quoted in various publications including The Associated Press, The New York Times, The Denver Post and ABC News. She has written for various magazines including Countryside and Small Stock Journal, Molly Green, Farm Show Magazine and Backyard Poultry Magazine. She holds an Engineering degree from an Ivy League from a previous life.

At its height, her previous homestead included over 100 chickens, geese and ducks, as well as cats, a dog, bees and a donkey named Elvis. She currently learning permaculture techniques to apply to her homestead in rural Oregon.

Learn more by visiting her site http://byjillb.com.

50454229R00050

Made in the USA
Columbia, SC
07 February 2019